'THE '50s

MELODY LINE, CHORDS AND LYRICS
FOR KEYBOARD • GUITAR • VOCAL

HAL•LEONARD®

ISBN 0-634-06418-5

Printed In Canada

HAL•LEONARD®
CORPORATION
7777 W. BLUEMOUND RD. P.O. BOX 13819 MILWAUKEE, WI 53213

Visit Hal Leonard Online at
www.halleonard.com

Welcome to the PAPERBACK SONGS SERIES.

Do you play piano, guitar, electronic keyboard, sing or play any instrument for that matter? If so, this handy "pocket tune" book is for you.

The concise, one-line music notation consists of:

MELODY, LYRICS & CHORD SYMBOLS

Whether strumming the chords on guitar, "faking" an arrangement on piano/keyboard or singing the lyrics, these fake book style arrangements can be enjoyed at any experience level – hobbyist to professional.

The musical skills necessary to successfully use this book are minimal. If you play guitar and need some help with chords, a basic chord chart is included at the back of the book.

While playing and singing is the first thing that comes to mind when using this book, it can also serve as a compact, comprehensive reference guide.

However you choose to use this PAPERBACK SONGS SERIES book, by all means have fun!

CONTENTS

(contents continued)

ALL I HAVE TO DO
IS DREAM

Words and Music by
BOUDLEAUX BRYANT

9

ALL SHOOK UP

Words and Music by OTIS BLACKWELL
and ELVIS PRESLEY

Medium Shuffle rhythm

A-well-a, bless my soul, what's wrong with me?__ I'm
hands are sha-ky and my knees are weak.__ I

itch-ing like a man __ on a fuz-zy tree.__ My
can't seem to stand __ on my own two feet.__

friends say I'm act-in' queer as a bug __ } I'm in
Who do you thank when you have such luck?__ }

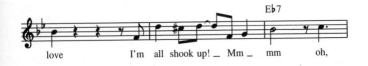

love I'm all shook up! __ Mm __ mm oh,

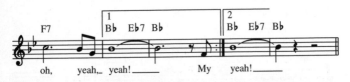

oh, yeah, yeah!_____ My yeah!_____

Please don't ask what's _ on my mind, _ I'm a
tongue gets tied when I try to speak, _ my _

lit - tle mixed up but I'm feel - in' fine. _ When I'm
in - sides shake like a leaf on a tree. There's _

near that girl that I love best, my
on - ly one cure for this soul of mine, that's to

heart beats so it scares me to death! } She
have the girl that I love so _ fine! }

touched my hand, what a chill I got, _ her

kiss - es are like _ a vol - ca - no that's hot! _ I'm

proud to say she's my but-ter-cup,. I'm in love! I'm

all shook up! — Mm — mm oh,

oh, yeah, — yeah! _____ My yeah! I'm

all shook up! _ Mm _ mm oh, oh, yeah, —

yeah! I'm all shook up! _ Mm _ mm oh,

oh, yeah, _ yeah! I'm all shook up! _

AUTUMN LEAVES
(Les Feuilles Mortes)

English lyric by JOHNNY MERCER
French lyric by JACQUES PREVERT
Music by JOSEPH KOSMA

The fall-ing leaves ___ drift by the win - dow, ___ the au-tumn leaves, ___ of red and gold. I see your lips, ___ the sum-mer kiss - es, ___ the sun-burned hands ___ I used to hold. Since you went a - way ___ the days grow long, ___ and soon I'll hear ___ old win - ter's song. But I miss you most of all my dar - ling, when au - tumn leaves start to fall.

AROUND THE WORLD
from AROUND THE WORLD IN EIGHTY DAYS

Words and Music by VICTOR YOUNG
and HAROLD ADAMSON

AT THE HOP

Words and Music by ARTHUR SINGER,
JOHN MADARA and DAVID WHITE

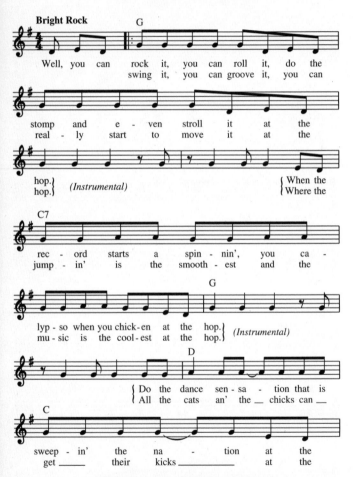

BLACK DENIM TROUSERS AND MOTORCYCLE BOOTS

Words and Music by JERRY LEIBER
and MIKE STOLLER

Briskly

He wore black den-im trou-sers and mo-tor-cy-cle boots and a black leath-er jack-et with an ea-gle on the back. He had a hopped-up cy-cle that took off like a gun. That fool was the ter-ror of high-way 1 0 1.

Well, he nev-er washed his face and he nev-er combed his hair. He had ax-le grease em-bed-ded un-der-neath his fin-ger-nails. On the

Lou, poor girl, she plead-ed and she begged him not to leave. She said, "I've got a feel-ing if you ride to-night I'll grieve." But her

had a hopped-up cy - cle that took off like a gun, That
could-n't find the cy - cle that took off like a gun, and they

fool was the ter - ror of high-way 1 0 1.

(Instrumental)

Mar - y nev - er found the ter - ror of

high - way 1 0 1.

BORN TOO LATE

Lyric by FRED TOBIAS
Music by CHARLES STROUSE

With a slow, driving beat

Born too late for you to no - tice

me, To you I'm just a kid that

you won't date, Why was I born too

late? Born too late to

have a chance to win your love, Oh

why, oh why was it my fate

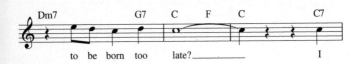

to be born too late?_____ I

see you walk with an - oth - er, I

wish it could be me; I

long to hold you and kiss you, But I

know it nev - er can be. For I was

born   too   late   for   you   to   care,   Now

my   heart   cries   be - cause   your   heart   just

could - n't   wait,   Why was I born too

late?   Why was I born   too

late?_____   Why   was   I

born   too   late?_____

BLUE SUEDE SHOES

Words and Music by
CARL LEE PERKINS

Bright tempo (not too fast)

Well, it's one for the mon-ey, two for the show, three to get read-y, now go, cat, go. But don't you step on my blue suede shoes. You can do an-y-thing but lay off of my blue suede shoes. Well, you can

knock me down, step on my face,
burn my house, steal my car,

25

BLUEBERRY HILL

Words and Music by AL LEWIS,
LARRY STOCK and VINCENT ROSE

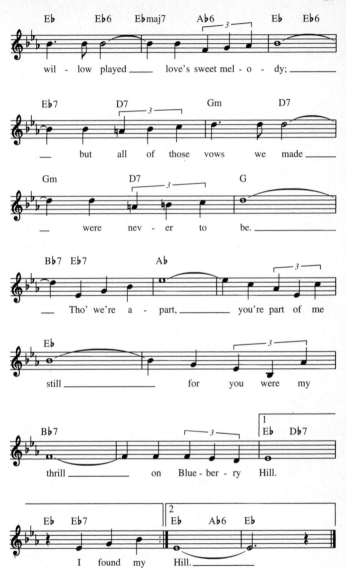

BORN TO BE WITH YOU

Words and Music by
DON ROBERTSON

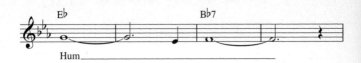

Eb   Bb7

Hum_____

Eb

Hum_____

Eb7   Ab

Hum_____

Abm   Eb   Bb7

Hum_____   Hum_____

Eb   1,2

_____

3   Ab   Eb

Hum   Hum_____

BYE BYE LOVE

Words and Music by FELICE BRYANT
and BOUDLEAUX BRYANT

CANADIAN SUNSET

Words by NORMAN GIMBEL
Music by EDDIE HEYWOOD

Moderately

Once,_____ I was a -
Cold,_____ cold was the

lone So_____
wind Warm,_____

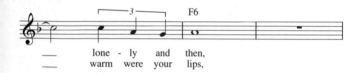

__ lone - ly and then,
__ warm were your lips,

you came,_____ out of
out there _____ on that

no - where,_____ like the sun _____
ski trail _____ where your kiss,_____

1 Gm7 C7

up from the hills.

filled me with

2 F6 Gm7

thrills._____ A week-end in

C9 Gm7 C7♭9 F F6

Can - a - da___ a change of scene

Gm7 D7♭9 C9 Gm7 C7♭9 C9 F6

was the most___ I bar - gained for.___

Gm7 C9 Gm7 C7♭9

And then I dis - cov - ered you___

F E7/B Am

and in your eyes I found a

34

love   that   I   could - n't   ig - nore.

Down,_____   down came the   sun

fast,_____   fast beat my   heart.

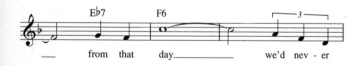

I   knew,_____   as   the   sun   set_____

_   from   that   day_____   we'd   nev - er

part.

CHANTILLY LACE

Words and Music by
J.P. RICHARDSON

CATCH A FALLING STAR

Words and Music by PAUL VANCE
and LEE POCKRISS

37

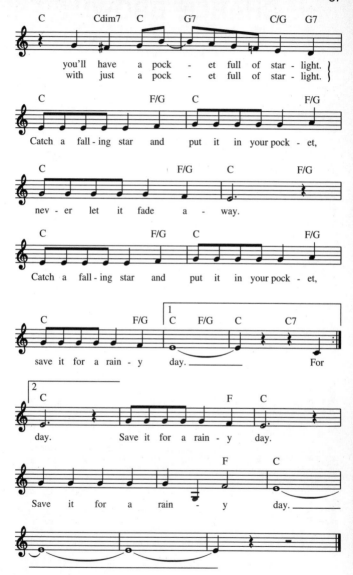

CHARLIE BROWN

Words and Music by JERRY LEIBER
and MIKE STOLLER

Medium bright Rock

Fee fee fi fi fo fo fum; I smell smoke in the

au-di-to-ri-um. Char-lie Brown. Char-lie

Brown, he's a clown, that Char-lie

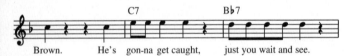

Brown. He's gon-na get caught, just you wait and see.

"Why is ev-'ry-bod-y al-ways pick-in' on me?" That's

him on his knees; I know that's him, __ yell-ing,

"Sev-en come e-lev-en" down in the boys'_ gym. Char-lie

COLD, COLD HEART

Words and Music by
HANK WILLIAMS

oth - er love be - fore my time made
was a time when I be - lieved that

C7

your heart sad and blue And so my heart is
you be - longed to me But now I know your

pay - ing now for things I did - n't
heart is shack - led to a mem - o -

F

do In an - ger, un - kind words are said that
ry The more I learn to care for you the

F7   Bb   C7

make the tear - drops start Why can't I free your
more we drift a - part Why can't I free your

1

doubt - ful mind and melt your cold, cold
doubt - ful mind and

2   F

heart? You'll melt your cold, cold heart?

COME FLY WITH ME

Words by SAMMY CAHN
Music by JAMES VAN HEUSEN

Moderately slow

When Dad and Moth-er dis-cov-ered one an-

oth-er, they dreamed of the day when they

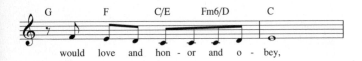

would love and hon-or and o-bey,

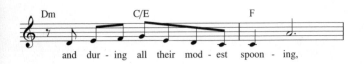

and dur-ing all their mod-est spoon-ing,

they'd blush and speak of hon-ey-moon-ing.

And if your mem-o-ry re-calls,

they spoke of Ni - ag - 'ra Falls____

____ But to - day, my dar - ling, to -

day, when you meet the one you

love, you say: ____ Come

Moderately, with a strong beat

fly with me!__ Let's fly!____ Let's fly__ a - way!__

____ If you can use __ some ex -

ot - ic booze,__ there's a bar in far Bom -
(views,) __

DANCE WITH ME HENRY
(The Wallflower)

Words and Music by HANK BALLARD,
ETTA JAMES and JOHNNY OTIS

48

Bb

F

— with me, Hen - ry.   Roll __ with me, Hen - ry.

C

Roll __ with me, Hen - ry. ___   You bet-ter

F

roll while the roll-in' is   on. Roll_ on, roll _ on, roll _ on. Well, _

I ain't teas-in'. (Talk_ to me babe.) You bet-ter stop your freez-in', (Al-

Bb

- right   ma-ma.) if you   wan - na ro - man - cin',

F

(O. K. sug - ar.)   you bet-ter learn some danc-in'.   Roll_

C

F

__ with me, Hen-ry. ___   You bet-ter roll it while the roll-in' is

D.S. and Fade

on. Roll __ on, roll __ on, roll __ on. You got to

COME GO WITH ME

Words and Music by
C.E. QUICK

CRYING IN THE CHAPEL

Words and Music by
ARTIE GLENN

You saw me cry-ing in the chap - el,
some - thing

the tears I shed were tears of joy.
that will put his heart at ease.

I know the mean-ing of con - tent - ment.
There is on-ly one true an - swer.

Now I am hap-py with the Lord.
He must get down on his knees.

Just a plain and sim-ple chap - el,
Meet your neigh-bor in the chap - el,

where hum-ble peo-ple go to pray:
join with him in tears of joy.

I pray the Lord that I'll grow strong - er,
You'll know the mean-ing of con - tent - ment,

G7 D7 G7 C F C F7

— as I live from day to day. ____
— then you'll be hap-py with the Lord. ____

C C7 F Fm6 Ab/Gb

I've searched and I've searched, but
You'll search and you'll search but

C A7 D7 Am7 D7

I could-n't find no way on earth to gain peace of
you'll nev-er find no way on earth to gain peace of

G7 N.C. F6

mind. Now I'm hap-py in the chap - el, ____
mind. Take your trou-bles to the chap - el, ____

C

— where peo-ple are of one ac - cord. ____
— Get down on your knees and pray. ____

A7 D7 Fm6/Ab

— We _ gath-er in the chap - el, ____
— Your _ bur-dens will be light - er, ____

G7 D7 G7 |1 C Dm7

— just to sing and praise the Lord.
— and you'll sure-ly find the

G7 N.C. |2 C F C F7 C

Ev-'ry sin-ner looks for way. ____

DON'T BE CRUEL
(To a Heart That's True)

Words and Music by OTIS BLACKWELL
and ELVIS PRESLEY

Medium bright (with a beat)

You know I can be found sitting home all a-lone if you can't come a-round, at least, please tel-e-phone. Don't be cruel to a heart that's true.

Baby, if I made you mad for some-thing I might have said please let's for-get the past the future looks bright a-head. Don't be cruel to a heart that's true. I don't want no oth-er love, Ba-by, it's just

you I'm think-ing of. _____

Don't stop think-ing of me, don't make me feel this
walk up to the preach-er, and let us say, "I

way. Come on o-ver here and love me, you
do." Then you'll know you have me, and I'll

know what I want you to say. Don't be cruel _____
know I'll have you too. Don't be cruel _____

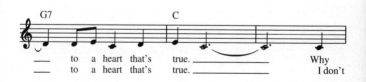

_____ to a heart that's true. _____ Why
_____ to a heart that's true. _____ I don't

should we be a - part? I real - ly love you,
want no oth - er love, Ba - by it's just

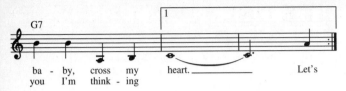

ba - by, cross my heart. _____ Let's
you I'm think - ing

of. _____ Don't be cruel _____

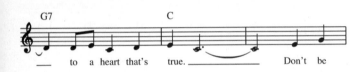

_____ to a heart that's true. _____ Don't be

cruel _____ to a heart that's true. _____

_____ I don't want no oth - er love

Ba - by, it's just you I'm think-ing of. _____

IT'S ONLY MAKE BELIEVE

Words and Music by CONWAY TWITTY
and JACK NANCE

Freely

People see us ev'ry-where,_ they think you real-ly care,_

but my-self I can't de-ceive, I know it's on-ly make be-

Slowly and steadily

lieve. My one and on-ly prayer,

is that some-day you'll care,__ my hopes, my dreams come true,

my one and on-ly you, no one will ev-er know,_

how much I love you so, my on - ly prayer will be,

some-day you'll care for me, but it's on - ly___ make_

_ be - lieve._____

My hopes, my dreams come true, my life I'd give for you,
My one and on - ly prayer is that some-day you'll care,

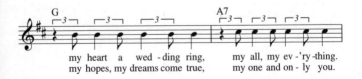

my heart a wed - ding ring, my all, my ev -'ry-thing.
my hopes, my dreams come true, my one and on - ly you.

My heart I can't con-trol,____ you rule my ver-y soul,____
No one will ev-er know,____ just how much I love you so,____

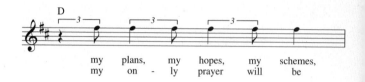

my plans, my hopes, my schemes,
my on-ly prayer will be

you are my ev-'ry-thing, but it's
that some-day you'll care for me but it's

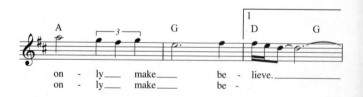

on-ly____ make____ be-lieve.____
on-ly____ make____ be-

____ lieve.____

DONNA

Words and Music by
RITCHIE VALENS

Repeat and Fade

EARTH ANGEL

Words and Music by
JESSE BELVIN

FEVER

**Words and Music by JOHN DAVENPORT
and EDDIE COOLEY**

1. Nev - er know how much I love you,
2. Sun lights up the day - time,
3.-5. *(See additional lyrics)*

nev - er know how much I care.
moon lights up the night.

When you put your arms a - round me, I get a
I light up when you call my name, and you

fe - ver that's so hard to bear. } You give me fe - ver
know I'm gon - na treat you right. }

when you kiss me,

Fe - ver when you hold me tight.

Fe - ver in the morn - ing,

Fe - ver all through _ the night.

night. Ev - 'ry-bod - y's got the fe - ver,

that is some - thing you all know.

Fe - ver is - n't such a new thing,

Fe - ver start - ed long _ a - go. burn.

Additional Lyrics

3. Romeo loved Juliet,
   Juliet she felt the same,
   When he put his arms around her,
     he said,
   "Julie, baby, you're my flame."

   Chorus:
   Thou givest fever, when we kisseth
   Fever with thy flaming youth.
   Fever - I'm afire
   Fever, yes I burn forsooth.

4. Captain Smith and Pocahontas
   Had a very mad affair
   When her Daddy tried to kill him,
     she said,
   "Daddy-o don't you dare."

   Chorus:
   Give me fever, with his kisses,
   Fever when he holds me tight.
   Fever - I'm his Missus
   Oh Daddy won't you treat him right.

5. Now you've listened to my story
   Here's the point that I have made.
   Chicks were born to give you fever
   Be it fahrenheit or centigrade.

   Chorus:
   They give you fever, when you kiss them
   Fever if you live and learn.
   Fever - till you sizzle
   What a lovely way to burn.

FLY ME TO THE MOON
(In Other Words)

Words and Music by
BART HOWARD

GET A JOB

Words and Music by EARL BEAL,
RICHARD LEWIS, RAYMOND EDWARDS
and WILLIAM HORTON

Moderately, with a rockin' beat

70

sha da da da da. And when I get ___ the ___
pa - per, I read it through and through, and
my { girl wife } nev - er fails to say ___
if there is an - y work for me. ___
___ And when I
go back to the house I hear the wom - an's mouth
preach - ing and a-cry-ing, tell me that I'm ly - ing 'bout a
job ___ that I nev - er could

GREAT BALLS OF FIRE

Words and Music by OTIS BLACKWELL
and JACK HAMMER

_ balls of fi - re! Kiss me, ba - by, Oh,

yo! It feels good. Hold me, ba - by.

I want to love you like a lov - er should_

you're fine,_ so kind._ I'm gon-na tell the world that you're

mine, mine, mine, mine. I chew my nails and I twid-dle my thumbs._

I'm real nerv- ous but it sure is fun! _

Oh, ba - by, you're driv- in' me cra - zy.

Good - ness gra - cious, great _____ balls of fi - re!

THE GREAT PRETENDER

Words and Music by
BUCK RAM

Moderately slow

Oh, yes, ___ I'm the great pre - tend - er, ___ pre -

tend-in' I'm ___ do-in' well. My need is such, ___ I pre-

tend too much; I'm lone - ly but no ___ one can tell. Oh,

yes, ___ I'm the great pre - tend - er, ___ a -

drift in a world ___ of my own. I play the game, ___ but to

my real shame, you've left me to dream ___ all a - lone. Too

real _____ is this feel - ing of make - be - lieve, too

real _ when I feel _ what my heart _ can't con-ceal. Oh, _____

yes, _____ I'm the great pre - tend - er, _____ just

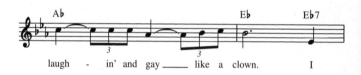

laugh - in' and gay _____ like a clown. I

seem to be _____ what I'm not, you see; I'm

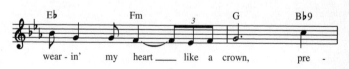

wear - in' my heart _____ like a crown, pre -

tend-in' that you're _ still a-roun'. Oh, roun'.

THE GREEN DOOR

Words and Music by BOB DAVIE
and MARVIN MOORE

Mid - night ___ one more night with - out
Knocked once ___ tried to tell 'em I'd

sleep - in'. ___
been there. ___

Watch - ing ___ till the morn - ing comes
Door slammed ___ hos - pi - tal - i - ty's

peep - in'. ___
thin there. ___

Green door ___ what's the se - cret you're
Won - der ___ just what's go - in' on

keep - in'. ___ There's an
in there. ___ Saw an

THE HAPPY WANDERER

Words by ANTONIA RIDGE
Music by FRIEDRICH W. MOLLER

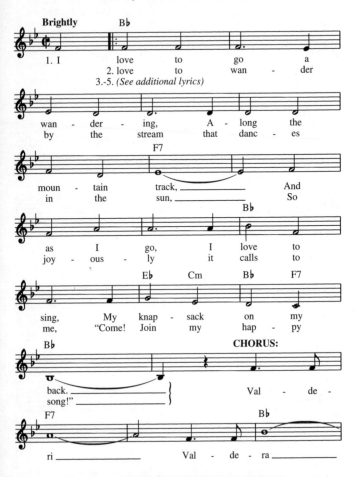

1. I love to go a
2. love to wan - der
3.-5. *(See additional lyrics)*

wan - der - ing, A - long the
by the stream that danc - es

moun - tain track, _____ And
in the sun, _____ So

as I go, I love to
joy - ous - ly it calls to

sing, My knap - sack on my
me, "Come! Join my hap - py

CHORUS:

back. _____ } Val - de -
song!" _____

ri _____ Val - de - ra _____

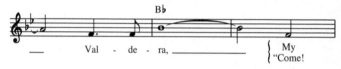

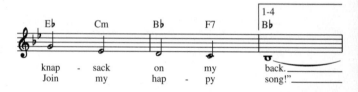

Additional Lyrics

3. I wave my hat to all I meet,
   And they wave back to me,
   And blackbirds call so loud and sweet
   From every greenwood tree.
   Chorus

4. High overhead, the skylarks wing,
   They never rest at home,
   But just like me, they love to sing,
   As o'er the world we roam.
   Chorus

5. Oh, may I go a-wandering
   Until the day I die!
   Oh, may I always laugh and sing,
   Beneath God's clear blue sky!
   Chorus

HAPPY, HAPPY BIRTHDAY BABY

**Words and Music by MARGO SYLVIA
and GILBERT LOPEZ**

HEARTBREAK HOTEL

Words and Music by MAE BOREN AXTON, TOMMY DURDEN and ELVIS PRESLEY

Blues tempo

Since my ba - by left me
If your ba - by leaves you and you

found a new place to dwell.
have a tale to tell,

Down at the end of Lone - ly
just take a walk down Lone - ly

Street at Heart - break Ho - tel. _____
Street to Heart - break Ho - tel. _____

Last time
fade here

I get so lone - ly ba - by.

I get so lone - ly.

I get so lone - ly I could

die. Al -

though it's al - ways crowd - ed,
Bell - hop's tears keep flow - ing,

still can find___ some room, where those bro - ken
desk clerks dressed_ in black. They been so

heart - ed lov - ers cry a -
long on Lone - ly Street they ain't nev - er

way their gloom, oh! } I get so lone - ly,
gonn' come back, oh! }

I get so lone - ly get so

D.C. and Fade

lone - ly I could die.

HEARTS OF STONE

Words and Music by EDDY RAY
and RUDY JACKSON

Moderately

F

Hearts made of stone _____ will nev - er

C   G7

break. _____ For the love you have for them, _____

G7#5   C   C7

_____ they just won't take.   You can ask them,

F   Dm7   G7   C

please, _____ please, please, please break _____

C#dim7   G7   G7#5
            3

_____ And all of your love _____ is there to

C   C7   F   Dm7

take.   Yes, hearts of stone _____

G7   C   C#dim7
                                              3

_____ will cause you pain, _____ Al - though you love

85

HEY, GOOD LOOKIN'

Words and Music by
HANK WILLIAMS

two dol - lar bill   and   I know   a spot right
o - ver   the fence   and find me __ one   for

o - ver the hill __   There's so - da pop and the
five or ten cents _   I'll keep it 'til it's __

danc - in's __ free, so if you wan-na have fun come a-
cov-ered with age ____ 'Cause I'm writ-in' your name down on

long with me __   Hey,   good   look - in'
ev - 'ry page _   Hey,   good   look - in'

What -   cha got cook - in'
What -   cha got cook - in'

How's a - bout cook - in' some - thin' up __ with
How's a - bout cook - in' some - thin' up __ with

1
me. ____   I'm

2
me. ____

HOUND DOG

Words and Music by JERRY LEIBER
and MIKE STOLLER

Medium bright Rock

You ain't noth-in' but a hound dog, ____

____ cry-in' all the time.

You ain't noth-in' but a hound dog, ____

____ cry-in' all the time.

Well, ____ you ain't nev-er caught a rab-bit and you

ain't no friend ____ of mine.

When they said you was high - classed,

well, that was just a lie.

When they said you was high - classed,

well, that was just a lie.

Well, __ you ain't nev - er caught a rab - bit and you

ain't no friend __ of mine.

You ain't noth - in' but a mine. _____

I ALMOST LOST MY MIND

Words and Music by
IVORY JOE HUNTER

Very slowly

1. When   I lost my ba - by   I
2. pass   a mil - lion peo - ple.   I

3., 4. *(See additional lyrics)*

al - most__ lost__ my mind.__
can't__ tell__ who__ I meet.__   I

When   I lost my ba - by.   I
pass   a mil - lion peo - ple.   I

al - most__ lost__ my__ mind.__   My
can't__ tell__ who__ I__ meet.__   'Cause

head is in a spin___ Since she left me be -
my eyes are full of tears. Where can my ba - by

hind._____ I
be?_____ I

Additional Lyrics

3. I went to see a gypsy, And had my fortune read.
   I went to see a gypsy, And had my fortune read.
   I hung my head in sorrow, When she said what she said.

4. I can tell you people, The news was not so good.
   Well I can tell you people, The news was not so good.
   She said your baby has quit you, This time she's gone for good.

I LEFT MY HEART
IN SAN FRANCISCO

Words by DOUGLASS CROSS
Music by GEORGE CORY

I left my heart in San Fran -

cis - co, _____ high on a hill,

it calls to me. To be where

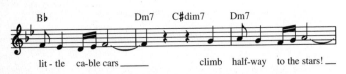

lit - tle ca-ble cars _____ climb half-way to the stars!

_____ The morn - ing fog _____ may chill the

air I don't care! My love waits there

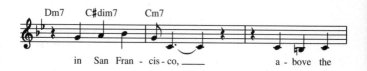

in San Fran - cis - co, _____ a - bove the

blue _____ and wind - y sea.

When I come home to you San Fran -

cis - co your gold - en sun will

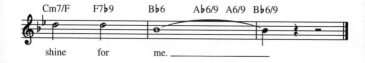

shine for me. _____

IT'S SO EASY

Words and Music by BUDDY HOLLY
and NORMAN PETTY

Moderately bright

It's so eas-y to fall in love,___

It's so eas-y to___ fall___ in love.___

Verse 1

Peo- ple tell me love's for fools,___ so

here I go___ break-ing all of the rules.___ It seems so

eas- y, so dog-gone eas- y;

It seems so eas-y, where

you're con-cerned._ My heart has learned; It's so eas-y to

fall in love,_ It's so eas-y to__

fall_ in love!_ fall_ in love!_

Verse 2

Look in-to your heart and see__

what your love book has set a-part_ for me. It seems so

IT'S SO NICE TO HAVE A MAN AROUND THE HOUSE

Lyric by JACK ELLIOTT
Music by HAROLD SPINA

Moderately slow

It's so nice to have a man a - round the
nice to have a man a - round the

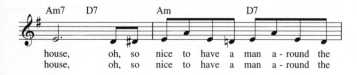

house, oh, so nice to have a man a - round the
house, oh, so nice to have a man a - round the

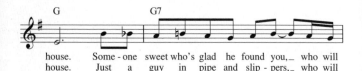

house. Some - one sweet who's glad he found you,_ who will
house. Just a guy in pipe and slip - pers,_ who will

put his arms a - round you.___ And his
share your break - fast kip - pers.___ And will

kiss - es just as - tound you, it's so
help you zip your zip - pers, it's so

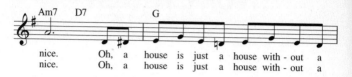

nice.   Oh,   a   house   is   just   a   house   with - out   a
nice.   Oh,   a   house   is   just   a   house   with - out   a

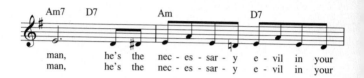

man,   he's   the   nec - es - sar - y   e - vil   in   your
man,   he's   the   nec - es - sar - y   e - vil   in   your

plan.   There   are   man - y   things   a - bout   him,   you   just
plan.   Some - one   kind   who   knows   you   treas - ure   an - y

can - not do with out   him, tho' it's   just   a   con - stant game of cat and
sim - ple lit - tle pleas - ure, like   a   full length mink   to   cov - er last year's

mouse,   It's   so   nice   to   have   a   man   a - round   the
blouse,   It's   so   nice   to   have   a   man   a - round   the

house.   It's   so   house.

IVORY TOWER

Words and Music by JACK FULTON
and LOIS STEELE

Moderate Waltz

Come down, come down from your i - vory
tow - er, { let love come in - to your heart.
{ you'll find true love has its charms.

Don't lock your - self in an i - vory
It's cold, so cold in your i - vory

To Coda

tow - er, don't keep us so far a - part.
tow - er, and warm, so warm in my

I love you, I love you.

Are you too far a - bove me to hear?

CODA

Bb7 **D.S. al Coda**
Come

Eb
arms.

KANSAS CITY

Words and Music by JERRY LEIBER
and MIKE STOLLER

Blues tempo

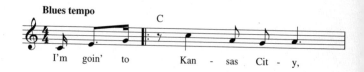

I'm goin' to Kan - sas Cit - y,

Kan - sas Cit - y, here I come

I'm goin' to Kan - sas Cit - y,

Kan - sas Cit - y, here I come.

They got a cra - zy way of lov - in' there and

100

JAILHOUSE ROCK

Words and Music by JERRY LEIBER
and MIKE STOLLER

Medium Rock

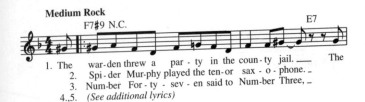

1. The warden threw a party in the coun-ty jail. ___ The
2. Spi-der Mur-phy played the ten-or sax-o-phone. ___
3. Num-ber For-ty-sev-en said to Num-ber Three, ___
4.,5. *(See additional lyrics)*

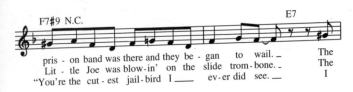

pris - on band was there and they be - gan to wail. ___ The
Lit - tle Joe was blow-in' on the slide trom-bone. ___ The
"You're the cut-est jail-bird I ___ ev-er did see. ___ I

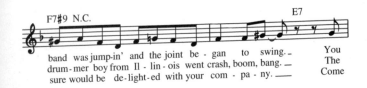

band was jump-in' and the joint be - gan to swing. ___ You
drum-mer boy from Il - lin - ois went crash, boom, bang. ___ The
sure would be de-light-ed with your com - pa - ny. ___ Come

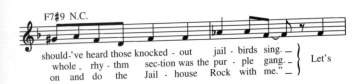

should.'ve heard those knocked - out jail - birds sing. ___ }
whole rhy - thm sec-tion was the pur - ple gang. ___ } Let's
on and do the Jail - house Rock with me." ___ }

rock!   Let's rock!

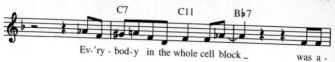

Ev-'ry - bod-y in the whole cell block _ was a -

danc-in' to the jail-house rock! _

Additional Lyrics

4. The sad sack was a-sittin' on a block of stone,
   Way over in the corner weeping all alone.
   The warden said, "Hey, buddy, don't you be no square.
   If you can't find a partner, use a wooden chair!"
   Let's rock, *etc.*

5. Shifty Henry said to Bugs, "For Heaven's sake,
   No one's lookin'; now's our chance to make a break."
   Bugsy turned to Shifty and he said, "Nix, nix;
   I wanna stick around a while and get my kicks."
   Let's rock, *etc.*

JUST IN TIME
from BELLS ARE RINGING
Words by BETTY COMDEN and ADOLPH GREEN
Music by JULE STYNE

Moderately

Just in time,____ I found you just in time.

____ Be - fore you came, my time____ was run - ning

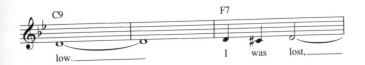

low.____ I was lost,____

____ the los - ing dice were tossed,____ My bridg - es

all were crossed,____ no - where to go.____

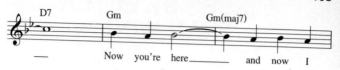

Now you're here_____ and now I

know just where I'm go - ing, no more doubt or fear,_____

_____ I've found my way._____ For love came

just in time._____ You found me just in time_____

_____ and changed my lone - ly life, that love - ly

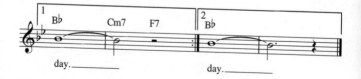

day._____   day._____

KISSES SWEETER THAN WINE

Words by RONNIE GILBERT, LEE HAYS,
FRED HELLERMAN and PETE SEEGER
Music by HUDDIE LEDBETTER

1. When I was a young man and
2. asked me to mar - ry and
3.- 5. *(See additional lyrics)*

nev - er been kissed, I got to think - in' o - ver
be his sweet wife, and we would be so hap - py

what I had missed. I got me a girl, I
all of our life. He begged and he plead - ed like a

kissed her and then, Oh, Lord, I
nat - ur - al man and then, Oh, Lord, I

Chorus

kissed her a - gain. }
gave him my hand. } Oh,

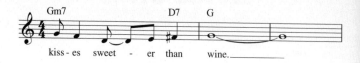

kiss - es sweet - er than wine.___

Oh,___ kiss - es sweet - er than

wine.___ He ___

Additional Lyrics

3. I worked mighty hard and so did my wife,
   A-workin' hand in hand to make a good life.
   With corn in the fields and wheat in the bins,
   And then, oh, Lord, I was the father of twins.
   Chorus

4. Our children numbered just about four,
   And they all had sweethearts knock on the door.
   They all got married, and they didn't wait.
   I was, oh, Lord, the grandfather of eight.
   Chorus

5. Now we are old and ready to go.
   We get to thinkin' what happened a long time ago.
   We had lots of kids and trouble and pain,
   But, oh, Lord, we'd do it again.
   Chorus

LITTLE STAR

Words and Music by ARTHUR VENOSA
and VITO PICONE

Oh,_____ ra - ta ta___ ta___

ta._____
Twin - kle, twin - kle,
Wish I may___
Searched all o - ver

lit - tle star.___ How I won - der
wish I might,_ make this wish come
for a love.___ You're the one I'm

Play 3 times

where you are.___
true to - night.___
think - ing of.___

Oh,_____

_____ ra - ta ta___ ta___ tu._____

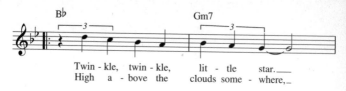

Twin - kle, twin - kle, lit - tle star.___
High a - bove the clouds some - where,_

How I won - der where you are.___
send me down a love to share._

Oh._____

— Oh there you are,_____
Oh there you are,_____

high a - bove.____ Oh____
hid - ing a - bove the sky,_

God,____ send me a love.____

I need a love,___ oh, me oh, me oh

my.___ Twin-kle, twin-kle, lit-tle star.___
Wish I may___ wish I might,___

How I won - der where you are.___
make this wish come true to - night.___

Oh,___ ra - ta

ta___ ta___ tu.___

Freely

Oh, ra ta ta oh.___

There you are, lit - tle star.

LOLLIPOP

Words and Music by BEVERLY ROSS
and JULIUS DIXON

Rock beat

Lol - li - pop, Lol - li - pop, Oh,___ lol - li, lol - li, lol - li,

Lol - li - pop, Lol - li - pop, Oh,___ lol - li, lol - li, lol - li,

Lol - li - pop, Lol - li - pop, Oh,___ lol - li, lol - li, lol - li,

Lol - li - pop.   *(Instrumental)*

Call my ba - by Lol - li - pop,   tell you why,
Cra - zy way she thrills - a me,   tell you why,

112

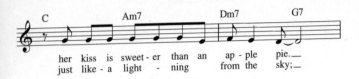

her kiss is sweet-er than an ap-ple pie.—
just like-a light - ning from the sky;—

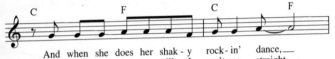

And when she does her shak-y rock-in' dance,—
She loves to kiss me till I can't see straight,—

man, I have-n't got a chance. } I call her
gee, my Lol-li-pop is great.

Lol-li-pop, Lol-li-pop, Oh,—— lol - li, lol-li, lol-li,

Lol-li-pop, Lol-li-pop, Oh,—— lol - li, lol-li, lol-li,

Lol-li-pop, Lol-li-pop, Oh,—— lol - li, lol-li, lol-li,

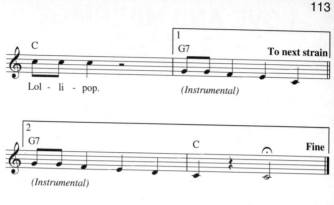

C

Lol - li - pop.

1
G7

(Instrumental)

To next strain

2
G7

(Instrumental)

C

Fine

F

Sweet - er than can - dy on a stick.___

C   F   C

Huck - le - ber - ry, cher - ry, or   lime;___

F

If you had a choice, she'd be your pick,___ but

D7   G7   **D.C. al Fine**

Lol - li - pop   is   mine._____   Oh,

LOVE AND MARRIAGE

Words by SAMMY CAHN
Music by JAMES VAN HEUSEN

Schottische tempo

Love and mar - riage, love and mar - riage,
Love and mar - riage, love and mar - riage,

Go to - geth - er like a horse and car - riage,
It's an in - sti - tute you can't dis - par - age,

This I tell ya broth - er, Ya can't have one with - out the
ask the lo - cal gen - try and they will say it's el - e -

oth - er. men - t'ry. Try, try,
try to sep - a - rate them, It's an il -

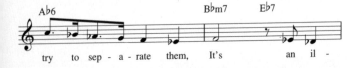

MEMORIES ARE MADE OF THIS

Words and Music by RICHARD DEHR,
FRANK MILLER and TERRY GILKYSON

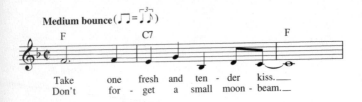

Take one fresh and ten - der kiss.
Don't for - get a small moon - beam.

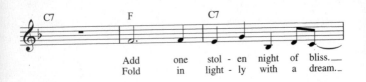

Add one stol - en night of bliss.
Fold in light - ly with a dream.

One girl,
Your lips

one boy: some grief, some joy.
and mine, two sips of wine.

Mem - o - ries are made of this.____
Mem - o - ries are made of this.____

Then add the wed - ding bells,__

one house where lov - ers dwell,_ three lit - tle

kids for the fla - vor.____

Stir care - f'lly thru the days;_ see how the

fla - vor stays_ these are the dreams you will

sa - vor. With His

bless - ings from a - bove,___

serve it gen - 'rous - ly with love.___

One man, one wife,

one love thru life, mem - o -

ries are made of this.___

PEGGY SUE

Words and Music by JERRY ALLISON, NORMAN PETTY and BUDDY HOLLY

Brightly

If you knew__ Peg - gy Sue,_
Peg - gy Sue,__ Peg - gy Sue,_

_ then you'd know why
_ oh, how my heart

I feel blue__ a - bout Peg - gy,__
yearns for you,__ oh, Pa - heg - gy,__

_ 'bout my Peg - gy Sue;
_ my Pa - heg - gy Sue;

Oh, well, I

love you, gal,__ yes, I love you,

120

MISTER SANDMAN

Lyric and Music by
PAT BALLARD

Boy: Mis - ter Sand - man
Sand - man

bring me a dream, ___ make her com -
bring me a dream, ___ make him the

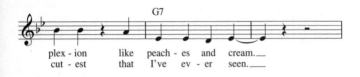

plex - ion like peach - es and cream. ___
cut - est that I've ev - er seen. ___

Give her two lips like ros - es in clo -
Give him the word that I'm not a rov -

- ver, then tell me that my lone - some
- er, then tell me that my lone - some

MOMENTS TO REMEMBER

Words by AL STILLMAN
Music by ROBERT ALLEN

Moderately slow, with feeling

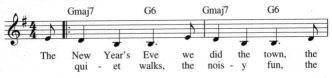

The New Year's Eve we did the town, the
qui-et walks, the nois-y fun, the

day we tore the goal-post down,)
ball-room prize we al-most won,)
we will have these

mo-ments to re-mem-ber. The

mem-ber. Tho' sum-mer turns to

win - ter and the pres - ent dis - ap - pears, the

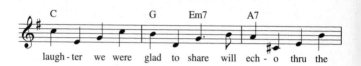

laugh - ter we were glad to share will ech - o thru the

years. When oth - er nights and oth - er days may

find us gone our sep' - rate ways, we will have these

mo - ments to re - mem - ber.____

MONA LISA

from the Paramount Picture CAPTAIN CAREY, U.S.A.

Words and Music by JAY LIVINGSTON
and RAY EVANS

Mo - na Li - sa, Mo - na Li - sa men have

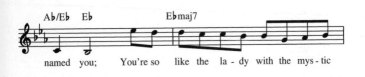

named you; You're so like the la - dy with the mys - tic

smile. Is it on - ly 'cause you're lone - ly ___ they have

blamed you for that Mo - na Li - sa strange-ness ___ in your

smile? Do you smile to tempt a lov - er, ___ Mo - na

Li - sa, _____ or is this your way to hide a bro - ken

heart? Man - y dreams have been brought to your

door - step. They just lie there, and they

die there. Are you warm, are you real, Mo - na

Li - sa, or just a cold and lone - ly love - ly work of

art? Mo - na art?

MY PRAYER

Music by GEORGES BOULANGER
Lyric and Musical Adaptation by JIMMY KENNEDY

Moderately

My prayer___ is to lin - ger with you___ at the end of the day___ ___ in a dream that's di - vine.___ My prayer___ is a rap - ture in blue ___ with the world far a - way___ and your lips close to mine.___ To - night___

OH! CAROL

Words and Music by HOWARD GREENFIELD
and NEIL SEDAKA

Moderately, with a rockin' beat

Oh! Car - ol, I am but a fool.

Dar-ling I love you though you treat me

cruel. You hurt me

and you make me cry. But if you

leave me, I will sure - ly die.

Dar - ling there will nev - er be an - oth - er

'cause I love you so._____ Don't ev - er

leave me; say you'll nev - er go.

I will al - ways want you for my sweet-heart,

no mat - ter what you do._____ Oh oh oh

Car - ol, I'm so in love with you._____

OH! MY PA-PA
(O Mein Papa)

English Words by JOHN TURNER
and GEOFFREY PARSONS
Music and Original Lyric by PAUL BURKHARD

Moderately slow, with expression

Oh! My pa - pa to me he was so
won - der - ful. Oh! My pa - pa to
me he was so good. No one could
be so gen - tle and so lov - a - ble.
Oh! My pa - pa he al - ways un - der -
stood. Gone are the days when he would take me
on his knee and with a smile he'd

OLD CAPE COD

Words and Music by CLAIRE ROTHROCK,
MILT YAKUS and ALLEN JEFFREY

Slowly, with expression

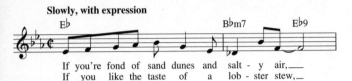

If you're fond of sand dunes and salt-y air,___
If you like the taste of a lob-ster stew,___

quaint lit-tle vil-lag-es here and there; }
served by a win-dow with an o-cean view; }

You're sure to fall in love with Old Cape

Cod.___ Old Cape

Cod.___ Wind-ing roads that seem to

PARTY DOLL

Words and Music by JAMES BOWEN
and BUDDY KNOX

(You've Got)
PERSONALITY

Words and Music by LLOYD PRICE
and HAROLD LOGAN

PICNIC
from the Columbia Technicolor Picture PICNIC

Words by STEVE ALLEN
Music by GEORGE W. DUNING

vous. _____ You and I in the sun-shine we

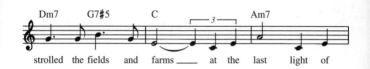

strolled the fields and farms ___ at the last light of

eve - ning, I held you in my arms. Now when

days grow storm - y and lone - ly

for me I just re - call pic - nic time with

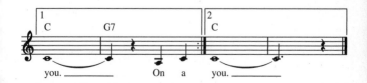

you. _____ On a you. _____

POOR LITTLE FOOL

Words and Music by
SHARON SHEELEY

Easy Rock

I	used	to	play	a - round	with	hearts	that
	play	a - round	and	tease	me	with	her
	told	me	how	she	cared	for	me,
	next	day	she	was	gone	and	I
	played	this	game	with	oth - er hearts but		I

hast - ened	at	my	call.	But
care - free	dev - il	eyes.		She'd
that	we'd	nev - er	part.	And
knew	she	lied	to	me.	She
nev - er	thought	I'd	see	the

when	I	met	that	lit - tle	girl	I
hold	me	close	and	kiss	me, but	her
so	for the ver - y	first	time		I
left	me	with	a	bro - ken	heart,	
day	when	some - one	else	would	play	love's

knew	that	I	would	fall,
heart	was	full	of	lies,
gave	a - way	my	heart,
won	her	vic - to - ry,
fool - ish	game	with	me,

poor lit - tle

fool, oh yeah._____

I_____ was a fool, _____ uh -

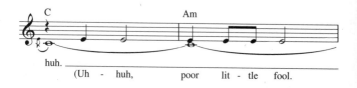

huh._____
(Uh - huh, poor lit - tle fool.

I was a fool, oh yeah.)
She'd
She
The yeah.)
Well, I've

yeah, oh yeah.)_____

QUE SERA, SERA
(Whatever Will Be, Will Be)

Words and Music by JAY LIVINGSTON
and RAY EVANS

Moderately bright

When I was just a lit - tle

girl, I asked my moth - er,

"What will I be?_____

Will I be pret - ty? Will I be

G7   Dm7   G7

rich?"   Here's   what   she   said   to

C   N.C.   F

me: "Que   se - ra,   se -

F6   F   F6

ra,_____   What - ev - er   will

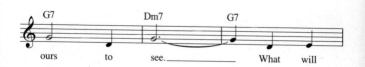

C   C6   C   C6

be,   will   be._____   The   fu - ture's   not

G7   Dm7   G7

ours   to   see._____   What   will

Dm7   G7   C   F   C

be,   will   be."_____

RAG MOP

Words and Music by JOHNNIE LEE WILLS
and DEACON ANDERSON

Rag   mop!   *(Instrumental)*

Bb7

Rag   mop!   *(Instrumental)*

F

Rag   mop!   *(Instrumental)*

C7

Rag   mop!   *(Instrumental)*

F   Bb

R - A - G - G.   M - O - P - P.

F   **D.C.**
                     (with repeat)
              1   C7   2

Rag   mop!   Mop! Mop!

RETURN TO ME

Words and Music by DANNY DI MINNO
and CARMEN LOMBARDO

Moderately

Re - turn to me, _____ oh, my dear, I'm so
me, _____ *non la scia - re mi*

lone - ly. _____ Hur - ry back, hur - ry back, oh my
so - lo; _____ *vien - i tu, vien - i tu, vien - i*

love, hur - ry back, I am yours. _____ Re - turn to
tu, vien - i tu, mi a - mor. _____ *Ri - tor - na a*

me _____ for my heart wants you on - ly. _____
me, _____ *ca - ra me - a ti a - mo;* _____

Hur - ry home, hur - ry home, won't you
so - lo tu, so - lo tu, so - lo

please hur-ry home to my heart?_____ My
tu, so - lo tu, mi - o cuor._____ Bam -

dar - ling,_____ if I hurt you, I'm sor - ry._____
bi - na,_____ dar il cour - a - nes su - no;

____ For - give me,_____ and please say you are
____ man - tie - ne,_____ so - la - men - te per

mine!_____ Re - turn to me,
me._____ Ri - tor - na a me,

____ please come back, bel - la mi - a._____ Hur - ry
____ e la - san - ta ve - nu - ta;_____ vien - i

back, hur-ry home to my arms, to my lips, and my heart.
tu, vien- i tu so - lo tu, so - lo tu mi a -

Ri - tor - na a mor!_____

ROCK AROUND THE CLOCK

Words and Music by MAX C. FREEDMAN and JIMMY DeKNIGHT

Moderately

One, two, three o'-clock, four o'-clock rock,

five, six, sev-en o'-clock, eight o'-clock rock,

nine, ten, e-lev-en o'-clock, twelve o'-clock rock, we're gon-na

rock a-round the clock to-night.__ Put your

SEARCHIN'

Words and Music by JERRY LEIBER
and MIKE STOLLER

Medium slow groove

(Gon - na find her) (Gon - na

find her) I been search - in',

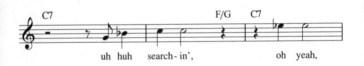

uh huh search - in', oh yeah,

search - in' ev - 'ry which a - way.

Oh yeah I been search - in',

search-in', search - in' ev -'ry

which_____ a - way._____ I'm like that

North - west Mount - ie, you know I'll

bring her in__ some day. (Gon - na

find her) Well now { if I have to / Sher - lock Holmes,

swim a riv - er you know I will.__ And
Sam Spade, got noth - in', child, on me,__

154

SH-BOOM
(Life Could Be a Dream)

Words and Music by JAMES KEYES, CLAUDE FEASTER,
CARL FEASTER, FLOYD McRAE and JAMES EDWARDS

Moderately bright

Life could be a dream, ⎫
Life could be a dream, ⎭ if I could take you up in

Par - a - dise up a - bove, If you would tell me I'm the

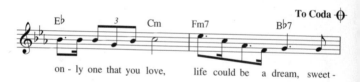

on - ly one that you love, life could be a dream, sweet -

heart. Hel - lo, hel - lo a - gain,___ Sh -

boom, and hop - in' we'll meet a - gain. Oh,

156

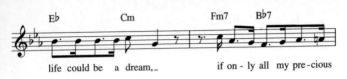

life could be a dream,— if on - ly all my pre - cious

plans would come true. If you would let me spend my

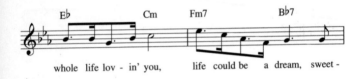

whole life lov - in' you, life could be a dream, sweet -

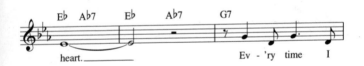

heart._____ Ev - 'ry time I

look at you__ some - thing is on my mind.__

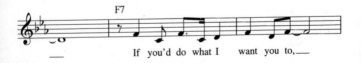

___ If you'd do what I want you to,—

ba - by, we'd be so fine.___ Oh,

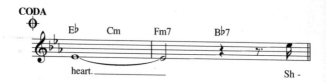

CODA

heart._____ Sh -

boom, sh - boom,___ ya da da da da da da da da da. Sh-

boom sh - boom,___ ya da da da da da da da da da. Sh-

boom sh - boom,___ ya da da da da da da da da da, sh-

boom. Sh - boom.

SECRETLY

Words and Music by AL HOFFMAN,
DICK MANNING and MARK MARKWELL

Slowly

Why must I meet you in a se - cret ren - dez-vous?
Why must we wait un - til we're danc - ing cheek to cheek

Why must we steal a way to steal a kiss or two?
to whis - per all the words of love we long to speak?

Why must we wait to do the things we want to do?
Why must our love be like a game of hide - and seek?

Why, oh why, oh why, oh why, oh why?

Wish we did - n't have to meet se - cret -

ly, wish we did - n't have to kiss se - cret -

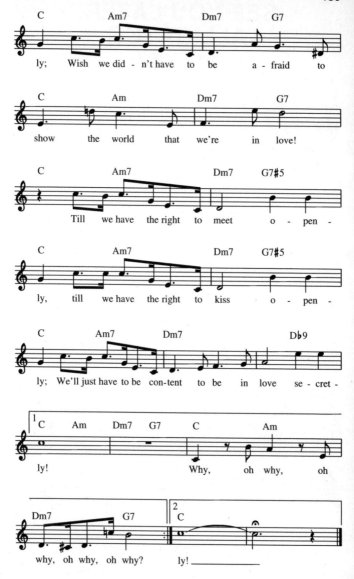

ly; Wish we did – n't have to be a - fraid to

show the world that we're in love!

Till we have the right to meet o - pen -

ly, till we have the right to kiss o - pen -

ly; We'll just have to be con-tent to be in love se - cret -

ly! Why, oh why, oh

why, oh why, oh why? ly! _____

SEE YOU LATER, ALLIGATOR

Words and Music by
ROBERT GUIDRY

Medium Shuffle

Well, I saw my ba - by walk - ing,
told me,

With an - oth - er man to - day,___
Near - ly made me lose my head,___

Well I saw my ba - by walk - ing,
When I thought of what she told me,

With an - oth - er man to - day,___
Near - ly made me lose my head._

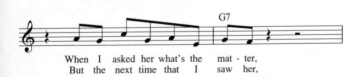

When I asked her what's the mat - ter,
But the next time that I saw her,

This is what I heard her say.)
Re-mind-ed her of what she said.)

See you lat-er, al-li - ga-tor,

Aft-er 'while,___ croc-o - dile;___

See you lat-er, al-li - ga-tor,

Aft-er 'while,___ croc-o - dile;___

Can't you see you're in my way, now?

Don't you know you cramp my style?

When I thought of what she style?___

SHAKE, RATTLE AND ROLL

Words and Music by
CHARLES CALHOUN

163

SHORT SHORTS

**Words and Music by BILL CRANDALL, TOM AUSTIN,
BOB GAUDIO and BILL DALTON**

Moderately

Boys: Who wears short shorts? *(Instrumental)*

Girls: We wear short shorts. *(Instrumental)*

Boys: Bless 'em, short shorts. *(Instrumental)*   *Girls:* We like short shorts.

(Instrumental)   *Boys:* Who wears short shorts?

(Instrumental)   *Girls:* We wear short shorts.

(Instrumental)

D.C. and Fade

SHRIMP BOATS

Words and Music by PAUL MASON HOWARD
and PAUL WESTON

Moderately

Shrimp boats is a - com - in', their sails are in

sight. Shrimp boats is a - com - in', there's

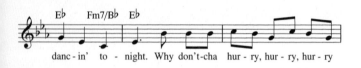

danc - in' to - night. Why don't-cha hur - ry, hur - ry, hur - ry

home, why don't-cha hur - ry, hur - ry, hur - ry home? (Look, here the)

Shrimp boats is a - com - in', there's danc - in' to -

night.   They go to sea with the
Hap - py the days while they're

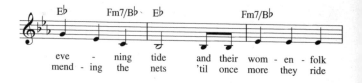

eve - ning tide and their wom - en - folk
mend - ing the nets 'til once more they ride

wave their good - bye._____
high out to sea._____

Ill____ sant vas, there____ they
Ill____ sant vas, there____ they

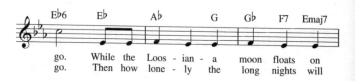

go. While the Loos - ian - a moon floats on
go. Then how lone - ly the long nights will

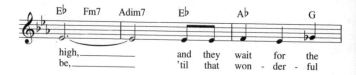

high,_____ and they wait for the
be,_____ 'til that won - der - ful

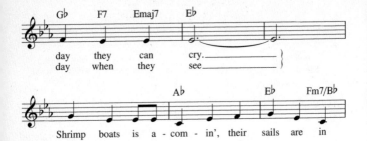

Gb   F7   Emaj7   Eb

day   they   can   cry._____
day   when   they   see_____

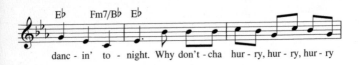

Ab   Eb   Fm7/Bb

Shrimp   boats   is   a - com - in',   their   sails   are   in

Eb   Ab

sight.   Shrimp   boats   is   a - com - in',   there's

Eb   Fm7/Bb   Eb

danc - in'   to - night.   Why   don't - cha   hur - ry,   hur - ry,   hur - ry

home,   why   don't - cha   hur - ry,   hur - ry,   hur - ry,

Ab

home?   (Look here the)   Shrimp   boats   is   a - com - in',   there's

Eb   Fm7/Bb   1. Eb   2. Eb

danc - in'   to - night.   night.

SINCERELY

Words and Music by ALAN FREED
and HARVEY FUQUA

Slowly, with a good beat

Sin - cere - ly,_____ Oh!_ Yes,_ sin -

cere - ly, 'cause I love you so_____

dear - ly,_____ please say_____ you'll be

mine._____ Sin - cere - ly,_____

oh, you know___ how I love you,

I'll do an - y - thing___ for___ you,___

___ please say___ you'll be mine.___ Oh,

Lord, won't you tell___ me why___ I

love___ that { fel - la / girl - ie } so,

{ he / she } does - n't want me.___ Oh, I'll

never, nev - er, nev - er, nev - er   let { him / her } go. Sin -

cere - ly,_____ oh, you know_ how I love you,

I'll do an - y - thing__ for__ you,_____

__ please   say_____ you'll be mine.

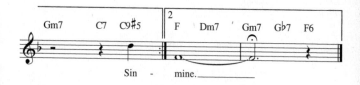

Sin - mine._____

SILHOUETTES

Words and Music by FRANK C. SLAY JR.
and BOB CREWE

Took a walk and passed your house late last
Lost con-trol, and rang your bell, I was

night, All the shades were pulled and drawn way down
sore, "Let me in, or else I'll beat down your

tight; From with-in a dim light cast two sil-hou-ettes on the
door." When two stran-gers, who had been two sil-hou-ettes on the

shade, Oh, what a love-ly cou-ple they made.___
shade said to my shock, "You're on the wrong block."_

Put {his/her} arms a-round your waist, held you
Rushed down to your house with wings on my

tight, Kiss-es I could al-most taste in the
feet, loved you like I've nev-er loved you my

night, Won - dered why I'm not the ⎰guy⎱ whose sil - hou - ette's on the
sweet, Vowed that you and I would be two sil - hou - ettes on the

shade I could - n't hide the tears in my eyes.
shade all of our days, two

Ah, _____

sil - hou - ettes on the shade. Ah _____

SINGING THE BLUES

Words and Music by
MELVIN ENDSLEY

Moderately

Well, I nev - er felt more like

sing-ing the blues_ 'cause I nev - er thought_ that

I'd ev - er lose_ your love, dear.

Why'd you do me this way?_____

_ Well, I nev - er felt more like

cry-ing all night_ 'cause ev-'ry-thing's wrong_ and

noth-ing ain't right_ with - out you.

You got me sing-ing the blues._____

— The moon and stars no

long - er shine, the dream is gone I

thought was mine. There's noth-ing left for

me to do but cry_____

o - ver you.___ Well, I nev - er felt more like

run - ning a - way___ but why should I go___ 'cause

I could - n't stay___ with - out you.

You got me sing - ing the blues.___

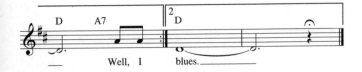

___ Well, I blues.___

STAGGER LEE

Words and Music by LLOYD PRICE
and HAROLD LOGAN

Freely

The night was clear and the moon was yel - low,___ and the

Moderate Shuffle

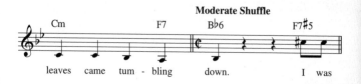

leaves came tum - bling down. I was

stand - ing_____ on the cor - ner_____ when I
Lee_____ told Bil - ly,_____ "I can't
Lee_____ went to the bar - room,_____ and he

heard my bull - dog bark. He was
let you go with that. You have
stood a - cross the bar - room door, Said, "Now

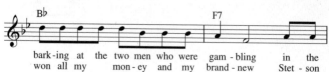

bark - ing at the two men who were gam - bling in the
won all my mon - ey and my brand - new Stet - son
no - bod - y move," and he pulled his for - ty-

SIXTEEN TONS

Words and Music by
MERLE TRAVIS

Moderately

Some peo-ple say a man is
born ___ one ___ morn-in' when the

made out of mud ___ A poor man's made out of
sun did-n't shine ___ I picked up my shov-el and I

mus-cle and blood Mus-cle and blood and
walked to the mine. I load-ed six teen tons of

skin and bones ___ A mind that's ___ weak and a
number nine coal And the straw-boss ___ said, "Well-a,

back that's strong. You load six - teen tons,
bless my soul." You load

what do you get? ____ An -

oth - er day old - er and

deep - er in debt. ____ Saint

Pe - ter, don't you call me 'cause

Am   Em

I can't go ___ I owe __ my soul to the

1.

com - pa - ny store. ____

2.

___ I was ____

SMALL WORLD

from GYPSY

Words by STEPHEN SONDHEIM
Music by JULE STYNE

SPLISH SPLASH

Words and Music by BOBBY DARIN
and MURRAY KAUFMAN

With a beat

Splish splash, I was tak - in' a bath
Bing bang, I saw the whole gang

'Long a - bout - a Sat - ur - day night.
Danc - in' on my liv - in' room rug.

A rub dub, just re - lax - in' in the tub,
Flip flop, they were do - in' the bop, all the

think - in' ev - 'ry-thing was all right. Well, I
teens had the danc - in' bug. There was

stepped out the tub, put my feet on the floor, I
Lol - li - pop with Peg - gy Sue, Good

wrapped the towel a - round me and I o - pened the door. And then
Gol - ly, Miss - Mol - ly was - a e - ven there too. A well - a

splish splash,   I   jumped back in   the   bath, _   well,
splish splash,   for - got   a - bout the   bath, _   I

how was   I   to know there was   a   par - ty   go - ing on?
went and   put   my   danc - ing shoes

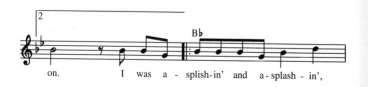

on.   I   was   a - splish-in'   and   a - splash - in',

I   was   a - roll - in'   and   a - stroll - in',

I   was   a - mov - in'   and   a - groov - in',

I   was   a - reel - in' with the   feel - in',   I   was a -

STANDING ON THE CORNER

from THE MOST HAPPY FELLA
By FRANK LOESSER

Stand-ing on the cor-ner watch-ing all the girls go by.

Stand-ing on the cor-ner
Stand-ing on the cor-ner
Stand-ing on the cor-ner

watch-ing all the girls go by.
giv-ing all the girls the eye.
un-der-neath a spring-time sky.

Broth-er you don't know a nic-er oc-cu-pa-tion mat-ter of fact neith-er do I
Broth-er if you've got a rich i-mag-i-na-tion, give it a whirl, give it a try
Broth-er you can't go to jail for what you're think-ing, or for the "wooooooo" look in your eye. You're on-ly

stand-ing on the cor-ner

watch-ing all the girls, watch-ing all the girls, watch-ing all the

girls go by._____ by._____

Fine

I'm the cat that got the cream,
Sat-ur-day and I'm so broke,

have-n't got a girl,__ but I can dream.
could-n't buy a girl,__ a nick-el Coke.

Have-n't got a girl,__ but I can wish, so I
Still I'm liv-ing like,__ a mil-lion-aire, when I

take me down to Main Street and that's where I se-lect my i-
take me down to Main Street and I re-view the ha-rem pa-

1st time: D.C.
2nd time: D.C. al Fine

mag - i - nar - y dish!
rad - ing for me here.

STUPID CUPID

Words and Music by HOWARD GREENFIELD
and NEIL SEDAKA

With a beat

Stu - pid Cu - pid, you're a real mean guy.__

I'd like to clip your wings so you can't fly.__

I'm in love and it's a cry - in' shame,__

and I know that you're the one to blame.__

Hey, hey, set me free.__ Stu - pid Cu - pid, stop

pick - in' on me. I can't do my home-work and I

can't think straight._ I meet him ev-'ry morn-in' 'bout a

Eb7 Ab

half past eight,_ I'm act-in' like a

Eb

love-sick fool._ You e-ven got me car-ry-in' his

Bb7 Ab7

books to school._ Hey, hey, set me free._

Eb N.C.

Stu-pid Cu-pid, stop pick-in' on me.

Ab Eb

You mixed me up but good_ right from the ver-y

Ab

start. Hey, go play Rob-in Hood_ with

some - bod - y el - se's heart.

You got me jump in' like a cra - zy clown,_

and I don't fea - ture what you're put - tin' down._

Since I kissed his lov - in' lips of wine,_ the

thing that both - ers me is that I like it fine._

Hey, hey, set me free._ Stu - pid Cu - pid, stop

pick - in' on me. pick - in' on me.

SUGARTIME

Words and Music by CHARLES PHILLIPS
and ODIS ECHOLS

Brightly

Sug - ar in the morn - in', sug - ar in the eve - nin',
Hon - ey in the morn - in', hon - ey in the eve - nin',

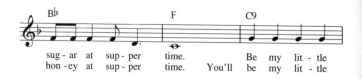

sug - ar at sup - per time. Be my lit - tle
hon - ey at sup - per time. You'll be my lit - tle

sug - ar_____ and love me all the time.___
hon - ey_____ and

love me all the time.___ Put your arms a -

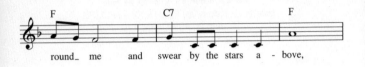

round— me and swear by the stars a - bove,

you'll be mine for - ev - er in a heav - en of

love. Sug - ar in the morn - in',

sug - ar in the eve - nin', sug - ar at sup - per

time. Be my lit - tle sug - ar_____ and

love me all the time.___ Now sug - ar time_____

___ is an - y - time,_____ that you're

near_____ or just ap - pear._____

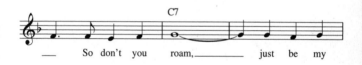

___ So don't you roam,_____ just be my

hon - ey - comb._____ We'll live in a heav - en of

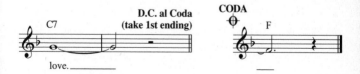

love._____

TAMMY

Words and Music by JAY LIVINGSTON and RAY EVANS

Slowly

I hear the cot-ton-woods whis-p'rin' a-
Whip-poor-will, whip-poor-will, you and I

bove: Tam - my! Tam - my!
know, Tam - my! Tam - my!

Tam-my's { my / in } love! The ole hoot - ie
Can't let him go! The breeze from the

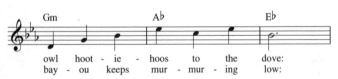

owl hoot - ie - hoos to the dove:
bay - ou keeps mur - mur - ing low:

Tam - my! Tam - my! Tam - my's { my / in }
Tam - my! Tam - my! You love him

195

TEACH ME TONIGHT

Words by SAMMY CAHN
Music by GENE DePAUL

Did you say I've got a lot to learn?____

___ Well, don't think I'm try-ing not to learn.

Since this is the per-fect spot to learn,

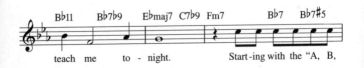

teach me to-night. Start-ing with the "A, B,

C" of it,———— right down to the "X, Y,

Z" of it, help me solve the mys - ter -

y of it, teach me to - night.

The sky's a black-board high a - bove you. If a

shoot - ing star goes by,———— I'll use that

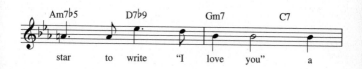

star to write "I love you" a

Cm7　　F9　　Fm7　　B♭7　B♭7♯5

thou-sand times a - cross the sky. One thing is - n't ver - y

E♭maj7　　A♭13　Gm7　　C7♯5

clear, my love.＿＿＿＿ Should the teach - er stand so

Fm7　　B♭7　Gm7♭5　　C7♯5

near, my love?＿＿＿＿ Grad - u - a - tion's al - most

Fm7　　B♭11　B♭7♭9　　1. E♭6　C7♭5

here, my love. Teach me to - night.

Fm7　　B♭7 B♭7♯5　　2. E♭6

Did you say I've got a night.＿＿＿＿

TEQUILA

By CHUCK RIO

201

(Spoken:) Tequila!

(Spoken:) Tequila!

THAT'LL BE THE DAY

Words and Music by JERRY ALLSION,
NORMAN PETTY and BUDDY HOLLY

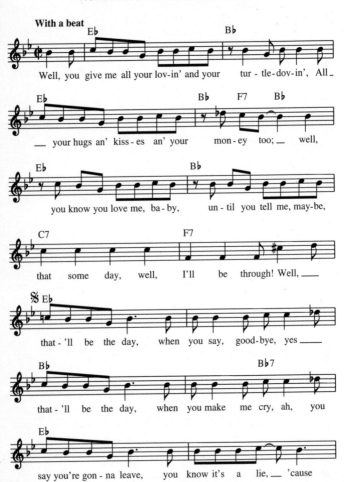

With a beat

Well, you give me all your lov-in' and your tur-tle-dov-in', All __ your hugs an' kiss-es an' your mon-ey too; __ well, you know you love me, ba-by, un-til you tell me, may-be, that some day, well, I'll be through! Well, __ that-'ll be the day, when you say, good-bye, yes __ that-'ll be the day, when you make me cry, ah, you say you're gon-na leave, you know it's a lie, __ 'cause

that-'ll be the day _____ when I die. _ Well,

_ when I die. _ when Cu-pid shot his dart,

he shot it at your heart, so if we ev-er part and

I leave you, you say you told me an' you

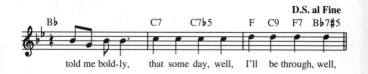

told me bold-ly, that some day, well, I'll be through, well,

THAT'S AMORÉ
(That's Love)
from the Paramount Picture THE CADDY
Words by JACK BROOKS
Music by HARRY WARREN

When the moon hits your eye like a

big piz - za pie, that's a - mor - é.

When the

world seems to shine like you've had too much

wine, that's a - mor - é.

Bells will ring, ting - a - ling - a -

ling, ting - a - ling - a - ling, and you'll sing, "Vee - ta

Db dim7

bel - la."_____

F7   Bdim7   F7

Hearts will play, tip - py - tip - py - tay, tip - py - tip - py -

tay like a gay tar - an - tel - la._____

Bb

___   When the

stars make you drool just like pas - ta fa -

Bb/D   Dbdim   F7   Bdim7

zool, that's a - mor - é._____

Cm7   F7

____ When you dance down the

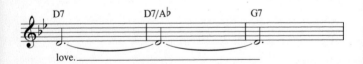

street with a cloud at your feet, you're in

D7   D7/Ab   G7

love._____

Cm

When you walk in a dream but you

know   you're   not   dream - ing,   Sig - nor -

é,_____   Scuz - za

me,   but   you   see,   back   in   old   Na - po -

li,   that's   a - mor - é._____

_____   When   the   mor - é._____

THE THREE BELLS

Words and Music by BERT REISFELD
and JEAN VILLARD

Moderately

There's a vil - lage hid - den deep in the
vil - lage hid - den deep in the
vil - lage hid - den deep in the
Vil - la - ge au fond de la val -

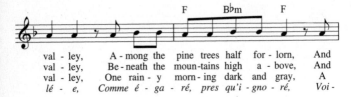

val - ley, A - mong the pine trees half for - lorn, And
val - ley, Be - neath the moun - tains high a - bove, And
val - ley, One rain - y morn - ing dark and gray, A
lé - e, Comme é - ga - ré, pres qu'i - gno - ré, Voi -

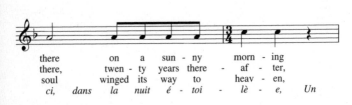

there on a sun - ny morn - ing
there, twen - ty years there - af - ter,
soul winged its way to heav - en,
ci, dans la nuit é - toi - lè - e, Un

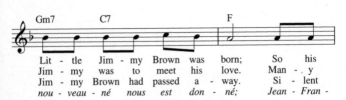

Lit - tle Jim - my Brown was born; So his
Jim - my was to meet his love. Man - y
Jim - my Brown had passed a - way. Si - lent
nou - veau - né nous est don - né; Jean - Fran -

F7 — **B♭**

par - ents brought him to the chap - el, When
friends were gath - ered in the chap - el, And
peo - ple gath - ered in the chap - el, To
çois Ni - cot___ il se nom - me, Il

G7 — **C** **C7** **F**

he was on - ly one day old, And the priest blessed the lit - tle
man - y tears of joy were shed, In June on a Sun - day
say fare - well to their old friend, Whose life had been like a
est jouf - flu, tendre et ro - sé, A l'é - gli - se, beau pe - tit

Gm7 **C7** — **F**

fel - low, "Wel - come, Jim - my, to the fold."
morn - ing, When Jim - my and his bride were wed.
flow - er, Bud - ding, bloom - ing till the end.
hom - me, De - main tu se - ras bap - ti - sé.

N.C. — **B♭**

All the chap - el bells were ring - ing
All the chap - el bells were ring - ing,
Just a lone - ly bell was ring - ing
U - ne clo - che son - ne, son - ne,

F

In the lit - tle val - ley town,
'Twas a great day in his life,
In the lit - tle val - ley town,
Sa voix d'é - chos en é - chos,

F7

And the song that they were sing - ing
'Cause the songs that they were sing - ing
'Twas fare - well that it was sing - ing
Dit au mon - de qui s'é - ton - nes

Was for ba - by Jim - my Brown.
Was for Jim - my and his wife.
To our good old Jim - my Brown.
C'est pour Jean - Fran - çois Ni - cot!

Then the lit - tle con - gre - ga - tion
Then the lit - tle con - gre - ga - tion
And the lit - tle con - gre - ga - tion
C'est pour accue il - lir une â - me

Prayed for guid - ance from a - bove,
Prayed for guid - ance from a - bove,
Prayed for guid - ance from a - bove,
U - ne fleur qui s'ouvre au jour;

"Lead us not in - to temp - ta - tion, Bless this hour of med - i -
"Lead us not in - to temp - ta - tion, Bless, oh Lord, this cel - e -
"Lead us not in - to temp - ta - tion, May his soul find the sal -
A peine, á peine, u - ne flam - me en - cor fai - ble qui rè -

ta - tion, Guide him with e - ter - nal love."
bra - tion, May their lives be filled with love."
va - tion Of Thy great e - ter - nal
cla - me Pro - tec - tion ten - dresse a -

There's a love.
From the *mour.*

TWEEDLE DEE

Words and Music by
WINFIELD SCOTT

Tweed - lee, tweed - lee, tweed - lee dee,__
Tweed - lee, tweed - lee, tweed - lee dot,__

I'm_____ as hap - py as can be;__
How_____ you're gon-na keep that hon-ey you got?__

Jim - i - ny Crick - ets, Jim - i - ny Jack. You
Hunk - ies hunk - ies, piec - es, bite,

make my heart go click - i - ty clack.
I'm gon-na see my hon - ey to - night.

Tweed - lee, tweed - lee, tweed - lee dee.___
Tweed - lee, tweed - lee, tweed - lee dot.___

Tweed - lee dee, tweed - le dee dee,___
Tweed - lee do, tweed - le dee do,___

Give it up, give it up,
Give that kiss to

give your love to me._____
me be - fore you go;_____

Tweed - lee dot, tweed - le dee dot,_____
Tweed - lee dum, tweed - le dee dum,_____

Gim - me, gim - me, gim - me, gim - me,
Look - ie, look - ie, look - ie, look - ie,

give me all the love you got.___)
look at that___ sug - ar plum.___)

Hum - ty, um - bum bum Tweed - lee,

tweed - lee, tweed - lee { do,_____
{ dum._____

I'm 'a luck - y so and so;____
You're as sweet as bub - ble gum;____

Hub - ba, hub - ba,
Mer - cy, mer - cy

hon - ey, do,____ I'm gon - na keep my
pud - din' pie,____ You've got some-thin' that

eyes____ on you,)
mon - ey can't buy,) Tweed - lee,

tweed - lee, tweed - lee { do.____
{ dum.__

THREE COINS IN THE FOUNTAIN

from THREE COINS IN THE FOUNTAIN

Words by SAMMY CAHN
Music by JULE STYNE

Moderately

Three coins in the foun - tain,
Three hearts in the foun - tain,

each one seek - ing hap - pi - ness,
each heart long - ing for its home,

thrown by three hope - ful lov - ers,
there they lie in the foun - tain,

which one will the foun - tain bless?
some - where in the heart of

Rome. Which one will the foun - tain

bless? Which one will the foun - tain

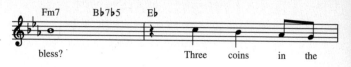

bless? Three coins in the

foun - tain, through the rip - ples how they

shine just one wish will be

grant - ed one heart will wear a val - en -

tine. Make it mine! Make it

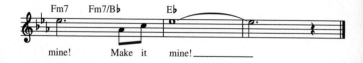

mine! Make it mine!_____

TILL THERE WAS YOU

from Meredith Willson's THE MUSIC MAN

By MEREDITH WILLSON

There were bells on the hill, but I
birds in the sky, but I

nev - er heard them ring - ing, no, I
nev - er saw them wing - ing, no, I

nev - er heard them at all till there was
nev - er saw them at all till there was

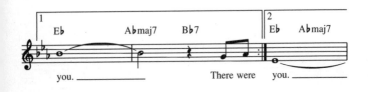

you. _____ There were you. _____

_____ And there was mu - sic and

there were won - der - ful ros - es, they

tell me in sweet fra - grant mead - ows of

dawn, and dew. There was love all a -

round, but I nev - er heard it

sing - ing, no, I nev - er heard it at

all till there was you.

TOM DOOLEY

Words and Music Collected, Adapted
and Arranged by FRANK WARNER,
JOHN A. LOMAX and ALAN LOMAX
From the singing of FRANK PROFFITT

Moderately

Hang down your head, Tom Doo - ley,

Hang down your head and cry,

Hang down your head, Tom Doo - ley, Poor

boy, you're bound to die.   I

met her on the moun - tain, And
This time to - mor - row,
This time to - mor - row,

TONIGHT YOU BELONG TO ME

Words by BILLY ROSE
Music by LEE DAVID

Moderately

Though you be - long to some - bod - y

else, To - night you be - long to

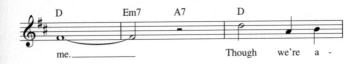

me._____ Though we're a -

part, you're part of my heart, to -

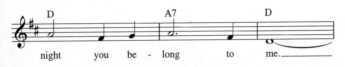

night you be - long to me._____

Down by the stream, how

sweet it will seem, Once more to

dream in the moon - light.____

Though with the dawn, I know you'll be

gone, to - night you be - long to

me.   me.____

221

TRUE LOVE

from HIGH SOCIETY

Words and Music by
COLE PORTER

Slowly

I give to you and you

give to me true

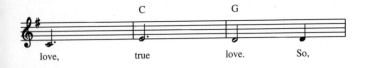

love, true love. So,

on and on it will al - ways

be true love,

true love. For you and

I have a guard – ian an – gel on

high with noth – ing to do ____

____ but to give to you and to

give to me love for –

ev – er true. ____

TUTTI FRUTTI

Words and Music by LITTLE RICHARD PENNIMAN
and DOROTHY LA BOSTRIE

Bright Rock tempo

A - bop - bop a - loom - op a - lop bop boom! Tut - ti

frut - ti   au   rut - ti,   tut - ti frut - ti   au

rut - ti,   tut - ti frut - ti   au   rut - ti,   tut - ti

frut - ti   au   rut - ti,   tut - ti frut - ti   au

rut - ti,   a   bop-bop a-loom-op a - lop bop boom! I got a

gal,   her name's Sue,   she knows just what to do...
gal,   her name's Dai - sy,   she al - most drives me cra -

UNCHAINED MELODY

Lyric by HY ZARET
Music by ALEX NORTH

Moderately slow

G — **Em** — **Cmaj7**

Oh, my love, my dar - ling, I've

D7 — **G**

hun - gered for your touch a

Em — **D** — **D7**

long, lone - ly time. _____

G — **Em** — **Cmaj7**

Time goes by so slow - ly and

D7 — **G**

time can do so much, are

Em — **Bm** — **D** — **D7**

you still mine? _____ I

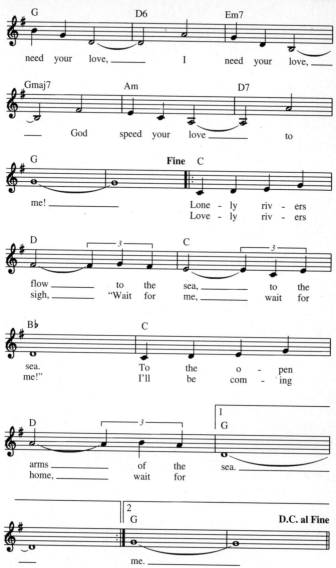

VENUS

Words and Music by
EDWARD MARSHALL

Moderately

Ve - nus, if you will,   please send a lit - tle
Ve - nus, make her fair,   a love - ly girl with

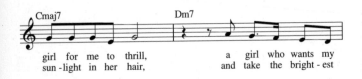

girl for me to thrill,   a girl who wants my
sun - light in her hair,   and take the bright - est

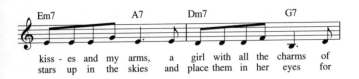

kiss - es and my arms,   a girl with all the charms of
stars up in the skies   and place them in her eyes for

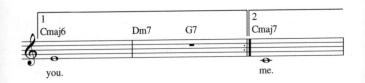

you.

me.

Fmaj7 / Dm7 / G7

Ve - nus,____ God-dess of love that you

Cmaj7 / Am7 / D7 / Gmaj7

are, sure - ly the things I ask

Am7 / D7 / Dm7 / G7

can't be too great a task.

Cmaj7 / Dm7

Ve - nus, if you do, I prom - ise that I

Cmaj7 / Dm7

al - ways will be true; I'll give her all the

Em7 / A7 / Dm7 / G7

love I have to give as long as we both shall

230

live.   Hey,   Ve -   nus,_____

_____   oh,   Ve -   nus,_____   make my wish come

true._____

Hey,   Ve -   nus._____

_____   Oh,   Ve -   nus._____   Hey,

WAKE UP LITTLE SUSIE

Words and Music by BOUDLEAUX BRYANT
and FELICE BRYANT

Moderately bright

Wake up little Su - sie, __ wake up.

Wake up little Su - sie, __ wake up.

We've / The

both been sound a - sleep, __ Wake up __
mov - ie was-n't so hot, __ it did -

__ lit - tle Su - sie, and weep. The
- n't have much of a plot. We

mov - ie's o - ver, it's four o' - clock __ and
fell a - sleep, our goose is cooked, __ our

WAND'RIN' STAR

from PAINT YOUR WAGON

Words by ALAN JAY LERNER
Music by FREDERICK LOEWE

star.   Mud can make you pris' - ner and the

plains can make you dry.   Snow can burn your eyes, but on - ly

peo - ple make you cry.   Home is made for com - in' from, for

dreams of go - in' to,   Which, with an - y luck will nev - er come

true.   I   was   born____   un - der a

wand' - rin'   star.   I   was

born____ un-der a wand' - rin' star.

When I get to heav-en, ___ tie me to a tree, ___ or

I'll be-gin to roam and soon__ you know where I will be.

I was born_____ un-der a

wand' - rin' star, A wand' - rin',

wand' - rin' star._____

WHY DO FOOLS FALL IN LOVE

Words and Music by MORRIS LEVY
and FRANKIE LYMON

Moderately fast

Oo - wah, oo - wah,__ oo - wah,__

oo - wah,__ oo - wah,__ oo - wah.__ Why__

___ do fools___ fall in love?__

Why do birds sing___ so gay___ and

lov - ers a - wait the break__ of day?__ Why__

___ do they fall_ in love?_____ Why__

___ does__ the_ rain_ fall__

___ from up a - bove? Why__ do fools_ fall__

___ in love? Why__ do they fall_ in love?__

{ Love_____ is a
{ Why_____ does my

los - ing game._ Love_ can be a shame. I know_
heart_____ skip a cra - zy beat? For_

__ of a fool,_ you see,_ for that
__ I know_ it will

fool   is   me. } Tell   me____   why.____

reach de - feat. }

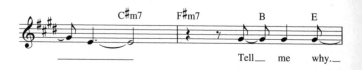

Tell____   me   why.____

Why____   do

fools   fall   in   love?____

WHEEL OF FORTUNE

Words and Music by BENNIE BENJAMIN
and GEORGE WEISS

Slowly and expressively

WONDERFUL! WONDERFUL!

Words by BEN RALEIGH
Music by SHERMAN EDWARDS

Moderately

Some - times we walk hand in hand by the sea and we
Some - times we stand on the top of a hill and we
Some qui - et eve - nings I sit by your side and we're

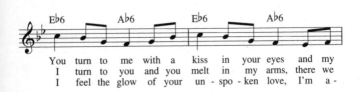

breathe in the cool salt - y air;
gaze at the earth and the sky;
lost in a world of our own;

You turn to me with a kiss in your eyes and my
I turn to you and you melt in my arms, there we
I feel the glow of your un - spo - ken love, I'm a -

heart feels a thrill be - yond com - pare! Then your
are, dar - ling, on - ly you and I! What a
ware, of the treas - ure that I own. And I

Gm   G7   Cm7   **To Coda**

lips cling to mine, it's won - der - ful! Won - der - ful!
mo - ment to share, it's won - der - ful! Won - der - ful!
say to my - self, it's won - der - ful! Won - der - ful!

1 B♭   C9   F7

Oh, so won - der - ful my love!

2 B♭   Cm7   F7   B♭

Oh, so won - der - ful my love! This

E♭maj7 E♭6 Fm7   B♭7   E♭

world is full of won - d'rous things, it's true, but they

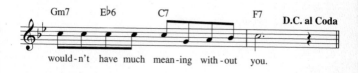

Gm7   E♭6   C7   F7   **D.C. al Coda**

would - n't have much mean - ing with - out you.

CODA

B♭   Cm7   F7   B♭

Oh, so won - der - ful my love!

YAKETY YAK

Words and Music by JERRY LEIBER
and MIKE STOLLER

Bright tempo

1. Take out the pa - pers and the trash,

2.- 4. *(See additional lyrics)*

or you don't get no spend - ing

cash. If you don't

scrub that kitch - en floor,

you ain't gon-na rock 'n' roll no more. Yak-et-y

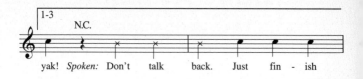

Additional Lyrics

2. Just finish cleaning up your room.
   Let's see that dust fly with that broom.
   Get all that garbage out of sight,
   Or you don't go out Friday night.
   Yakety yak! *Spoken:* Don't talk back.

3. You just put on your coat and hat.
   And walk yourself to the laundrymat.
   And when you finish doing that,
   Bring in the dog and put out the cat.
   Yakety yak! *Spoken:* Don't talk back.

4. Don't you give me no dirty looks.
   Your father's hip; he knows what cooks.
   Just tell your hoodlum friend outside,
   You ain't got time to take a ride.
   Yakety yak! *Spoken:* Don't talk back.
   Yakety yak, Yakety yak!

YOUNG AT HEART

Words by CAROLYN LEIGH
Music by JOHNNY RICHARDS

Slowly

Fair - y tales___ can come true,___ it can
know___ that it's worth___ ev - 'ry

hap - pen to you if you're young at heart.___
treas - ure on earth to be young at heart?___

___ For it's hard,___ you will find,___ to be
___ For as rich___ as you are,___ it's much

nar - row of mind if you're young at heart.___
bet - ter by far to be young at heart.___

___ You can go___ to ex - tremes___ with im -
___ And if you___ should sur - vive___ to a

pos - si - ble schemes, you can laugh_ when your dreams_ fall a-
hun-dred and five look at all__ you'll de - rive__ out of

part at the seams and life gets more ex - cit - ing with each

pass - ing day,__ and love is ei - ther in your heart or

on the way.__ Don't you be-ing a - live, and

here is the best part,__ you have a head start__

if you are a - mong the ver - y young at heart.__

YOUNG LOVE

Words and Music by
RIC CARTEY

Moderately

They say for ev - 'ry boy and girl there's
Just one kiss from your sweet lips will

just one love in this old world, and I___ know___
tell me that your love is real, and I_____ can

I've_____ found mine._____ The
feel___ that it's true._____

heav - en - ly touch of your em - brace tells
We will vow to one an - oth - er

me no one can take your place
there will nev - er be an - oth - er

ev - er___ in my heart.___
love___ for you___ or for me.___

___ } Young love, first love,___

filled with true___ de - vo - tion.___

___ Young love, our love___ we

share with deep___ e - mo - tion.___

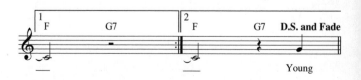

___ ___ Young

YOUR CHEATIN' HEART

Words and Music by
HANK WILLIAMS

Moderately

Your cheat-in' heart ___ will make you
heart ___ will pine some

weep ___ You'll cry and ___ cry ___
day ___ And crave the ___ love ___

___ and try to sleep ___ But sleep won't ___
___ you threw a-way ___ The time will ___

come ___ the whole night through ___
come ___ when you'll be blue ___

___ } Your cheat-in' ___ heart ___ will tell on

you _____ When tears come down _____

___ like fall - in' rain _____ You'll toss a -

round _____ and call my name _____

___ You'll walk the ___ floor _____ the way I

do _____ Your cheat - in' ___

heart _____ will tell on you. _____

___ Your cheat - in' ___ you. _____

GUITAR CHORD FRAMES

	C	Cm	C+	C6	Cm6
C					
	C#	C#m	C#+	C#6	C#m6
C#/Db					
	D	Dm	D+	D6	Dm6
D					
	Eb	Ebm	Eb+	Eb6	Ebm6
Eb/D#					
	E	Em	E+	E6	Em6
E					
	F	Fm	F+	F6	Fm6
F					

This guitar chord reference includes 120 commonly used chords. For a more complete guide to guitar chords, see "THE PAPERBACK CHORD BOOK" (HL00702009).

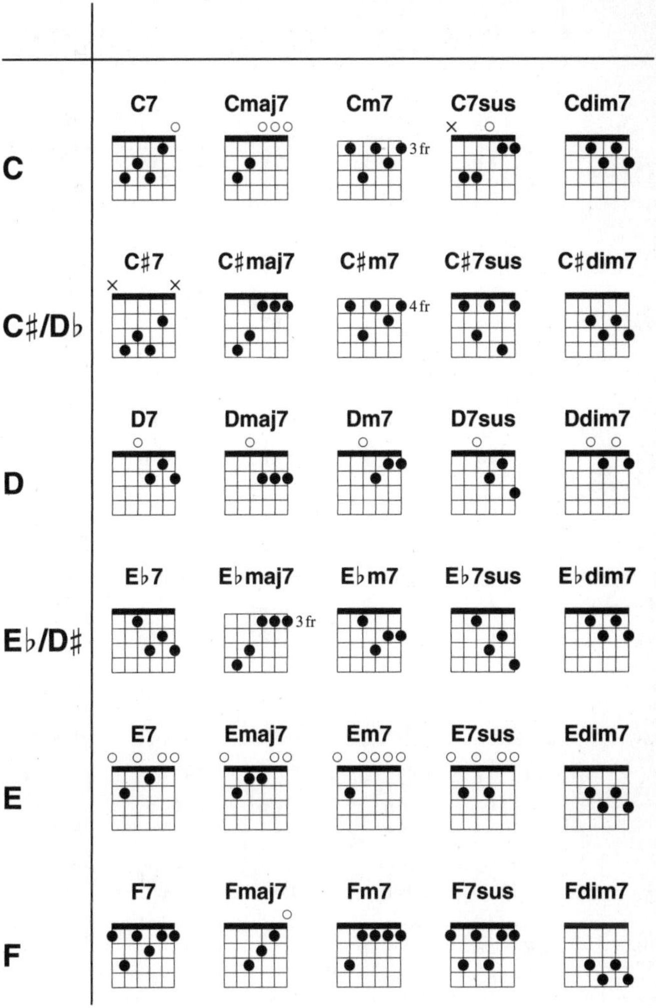
C
C7
Cmaj7
Cm7
3 fr
C7sus
Cdim7
C♯/D♭
C♯7
C♯maj7
C♯m7
4 fr
C♯7sus
C♯dim7
D
D7
Dmaj7
Dm7
D7sus
Ddim7
E♭/D♯
E♭7
E♭maj7
3 fr
E♭m7
E♭7sus
E♭dim7
E
E7
Emaj7
Em7
E7sus
Edim7
F
F7
Fmaj7
Fm7
F7sus
Fdim7

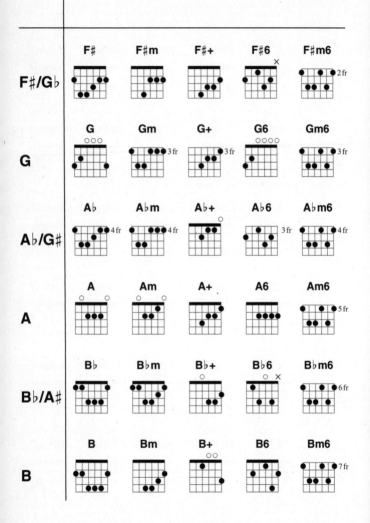

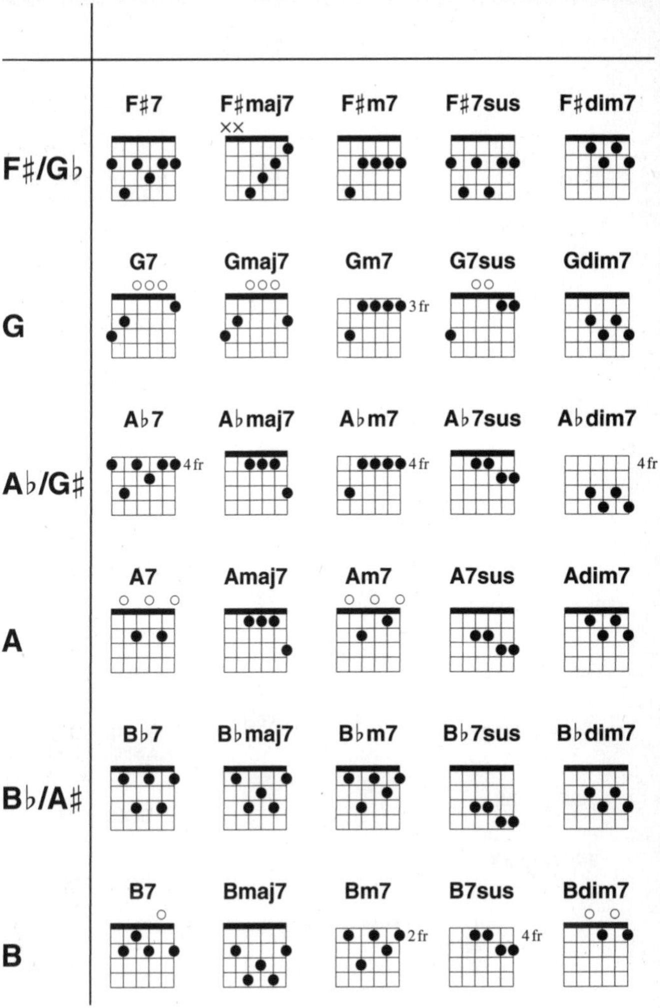
F♯/G♭
F♯7
F♯maj7
F♯m7
F♯7sus
F♯dim7
G
G7
Gmaj7
Gm7
3 fr
G7sus
Gdim7
A♭/G♯
A♭7
4 fr
A♭maj7
A♭m7
4 fr
A♭7sus
A♭dim7
4 fr
A
A7
Amaj7
Am7
A7sus
Adim7
B♭/A♯
B♭7
B♭maj7
B♭m7
B♭7sus
B♭dim7
B
B7
Bmaj7
Bm7
2 fr
B7sus
4 fr
Bdim7

THE PAPERBACK SONGS SERIES

$7.95 EACH

THE '20s
00240236

THE '30s
00240238

THE '40s
00240239

THE '50s
00240240

THE '60s
00240241

THE '70s
00240242

THE '80s
00240243

THE '90s
00240244

'80s & '90s ROCK
00240126

THE BEATLES
00702008

BIG BAND SWING
00240171

THE BLUES
00702014

BROADWAY SONGS
00240157

CHILDREN'S SONGS
00240149

CHORDS FOR KEYBOARD & GUITAR
00702009

CHRISTMAS CAROLS
00240142

CHRISTMAS SONGS
00240208

CLASSIC ROCK
00310058

CLASSICAL THEMES
00240160

COUNTRY HITS
00702013

NEIL DIAMOND
00702012

GOOD OL' SONGS
00240159

GOSPEL SONGS
00240143

HYMNS
00240103

INTERNATIONAL FOLKSONGS
00240104

JAZZ STANDARDS
00240114

LATIN SONGS
00240156

LOVE SONGS
00240150

MOTOWN HITS
00240125

MOVIE MUSIC
00240113

POP/ROCK
00240179

ELVIS PRESLEY
00240102

THE ROCK & ROLL COLLECTION
00702020

RODGERS & HAMMERSTEIN
00240177

SOUL HITS
00240178

TV THEMES
00240170